Searchlight
BOOKS™

What's
Amazing
about Space?

Exploring
Space
Travel

Laura Hamilton Waxman

Lerner Publications Company
Minneapolis

Lerner Publications Company
A division of Lerner Publishing Group, Inc.
241 First Avenue North
Minneapolis, MN 55401 U.S.A.

Website address: www.lernerbooks.com

Library of Congress Cataloging-in-Publication Data

Waxman, Laura Hamilton, author.
    Exploring space travel / by Laura Hamilton Waxman.
       p.   cm. — (Searchlight Books™—What's amazing about space?)
    Includes index.
    ISBN 978–0–7613–5447–5 (lib. bdg. : alk. paper)
    1. Manned spaceflight—Juvenile literature. I. Title.
  TL873.W39 2012
  629.45—dc22   2010042471

Manufactured in the United States of America
4 – CW – 4/1/15

Contents

Chapter 1

LEAVING EARTH

Imagine strapping yourself in for a flight. In front of you are computer screens and a control panel. A voice counts down to zero. Rockets fire. Your trip into space is about to begin.

The space shuttle *Endeavour* blasts off. Who was the first person in space?

Spaceflight

People have traveled in spacecraft for more than fifty years. Spacecraft take people and supplies into space. A Russian named Yuri Gagarin was the first person to fly into space. Gagarin's flight took place in 1961. It lasted 108 minutes.

Russian Yuri Gagarin was the first person to go to space. He is shown here before his 1961 flight.

Since then, people have taken much longer trips to space. Spacecraft have taken people around Earth and to the Moon.

Buzz Aldrin, pictured here, visited the Moon in 1969.

Space Travelers

Astronauts travel to space. These people fly spacecraft. They build and fix space equipment. They also run the International Space Station (ISS). This large space station flies 240 miles (386 kilometers) above Earth. Astronauts from around the world live and work there.

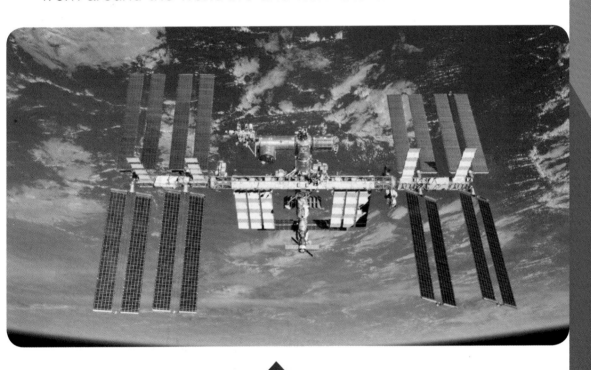

THE INTERNATIONAL SPACE STATION
CIRCLES HIGH ABOVE EARTH.

Chapter 2

SPACECRAFT

Throw a ball up to the sky. What happens? Earth's gravity pulls it back down. Gravity is the force that pulls objects together. Gravity keeps everything on Earth from floating away.

Space shuttle *Discovery* returns to Earth. What force pulls it toward the ground?

This side view of a space shuttle lifting off shows the rockets attached to the shuttle.

Roaring Rockets

Spacecraft need powerful rockets to break free of Earth's gravity. The rockets launch spacecraft toward space with great force. They drop away after their job is done. Then the spacecraft's engines take over.

The Space Shuttle

Many astronauts have flown in space shuttles. These U.S. spacecraft were shot straight up into the air. They landed back on Earth like an airplane.

Astronauts used shuttles for thirty years. But these machines got too old to fly safely. They stopped going to space in 2011.

A parachute trails behind space shuttle *Atlantis* as it lands. The parachute helps the shuttle slow down after it lands.

Other Spacecraft

In the past, the United States and other countries built their own spacecraft. Recently, private companies such as SpaceX have built spacecraft. These spacecraft are for carrying supplies into space. Someday they may carry astronauts too.

SpaceX launched a spacecraft in 2010.

Modern astronauts fly in Russian spacecraft called Soyuz. A Soyuz has three main sections called modules. Astronauts squeeze into the middle module for takeoff and landing. This module is called the reentry module. It has computers and controls for the spacecraft. Astronauts climb into the top module for the rest of the flight. It has a toilet, a sleeping area, and food. The bottom module holds supplies.

A Russian Soyuz circles Earth.

Taking Off

The Soyuz is fast. It takes about nine minutes to go from Earth into space. A car on a highway would take about two hours to travel the same distance.

A Soyuz spacecraft blasts off with astronauts headed to the ISS.

These astronauts are strapped into a Soyuz. They will feel high g-forces when they blast off.

Astronauts must deal with high g-forces. G-forces are the feeling of weight caused when a spacecraft speeds up very quickly. High g-forces make astronauts feel as if gravity is pressing down on them. One astronaut said it feels as if a gorilla is sitting on his chest! Breathing, moving, and even swallowing can be hard.

The spacecraft stops gaining speed once it enters space. Then the g-forces go away. The astronauts become weightless. They no longer feel the pull of gravity. They float about the spacecraft freely. Loose objects float around too!

This ISS astronaut shows off a model of part of the station. The astronaut and the model float because everything in space is weightless.

Returning Home

Returning to Earth in a Soyuz is a lot like falling. The reentry module breaks away from the rest of the spacecraft. It falls through the sky at great speeds.

This is the reentry module for the Soyuz. Astronauts use it to return to Earth.

The speeding module rubs up against the air. This rubbing creates a force called friction. The friction between the module and the air creates heat. A heat shield protects the reentry module. The module has a parachute to help it land safely.

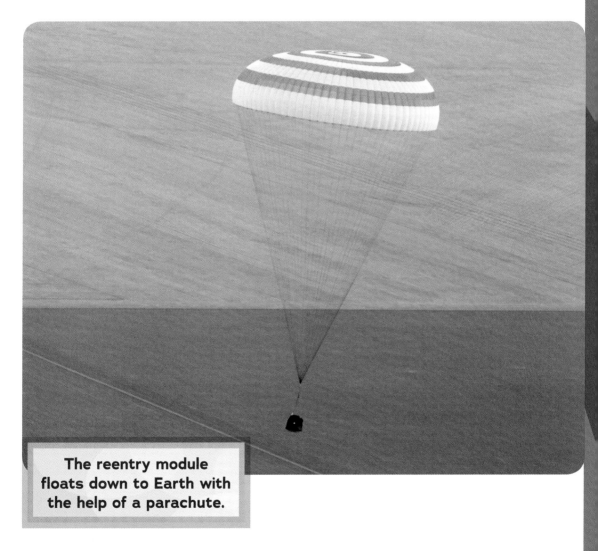

The reentry module floats down to Earth with the help of a parachute.

Chapter 3

SPACE GEAR

Astronauts strap themselves to their seats for takeoff and landing. But they need more than seat belts to stay safe.

Astronauts get help strapping into the space shuttle. How do they keep safe while in space?

Dressed for Flight

Astronauts wear flight suits during takeoff and landing. Flight suits cover astronauts from head to toe. An inner layer is made of a tight rubbery material. The outer layer is made of fire-resistant fabric. It protects astronauts from heat and flames.

American and Russian astronauts pose for a photo in their flight suits.

Flight suits also protect astronauts from a loss of air pressure. Air pressure is caused by air pressing against our bodies. The human body is made to live at Earth's air pressure. It can't survive in space, where there is no air pressure. Normally a spacecraft keeps a safe air pressure for the crew. But a flight suit could take over this job for a short time.

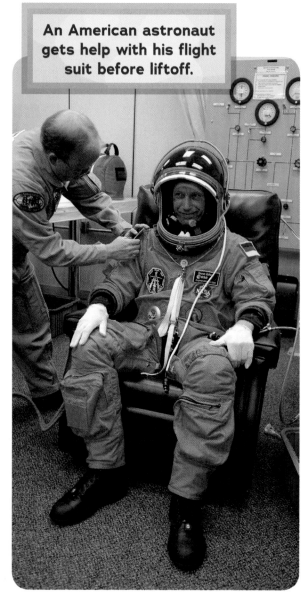

An American astronaut gets help with his flight suit before liftoff.

Space Suits

Astronauts sometimes work outside a spacecraft. This is called a space walk.

Astronauts on a space walk wear space suits. A space suit is made of fourteen layers. It gives the astronaut air pressure. It stays at a safe temperature. It blocks the Sun's harmful rays. It even stops small bits of fast-moving rock and dust from hurting the astronaut.

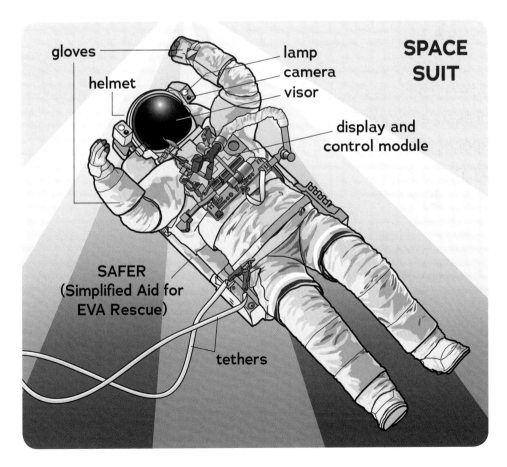

gloves

helmet

lamp
camera
visor

display and
control module

SPACE SUIT

SAFER
(Simplified Aid for
EVA Rescue)

tethers

Breathing Easy

Space suits also supply oxygen. People need this gas to breathe. Space doesn't have any air. So astronauts carry oxygen tanks on their backs. The oxygen flows from the tanks into a hard helmet.

A space suit protects this astronaut while he works on the ISS during a space walk.

Being Safe

Astronauts on space walks also wear a SAFER. SAFER stands for Simplified Aid for EVA Rescue. EVA stands for extravehicular activity. SAFERs are flying machines. They fit like backpacks. Their small jets can move an astronaut short distances. But astronauts usually stay tied to one place. Otherwise, they would float away.

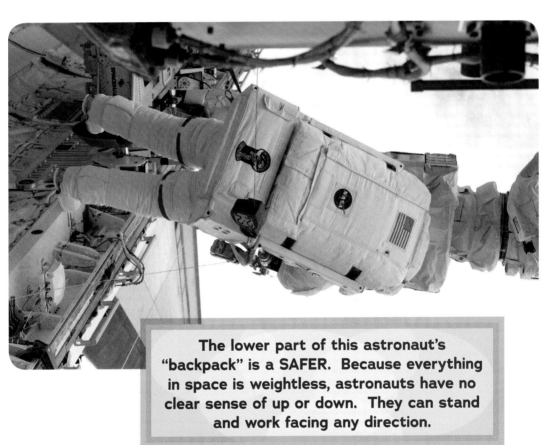

The lower part of this astronaut's "backpack" is a SAFER. Because everything in space is weightless, astronauts have no clear sense of up or down. They can stand and work facing any direction.

Chapter 4

LIFE IN SPACE

A spacecraft carries everything astronauts need. It stores food, water, and equipment. It is filled with air. Astronauts don't need helmets or special suits to breathe in a spacecraft.

Astronauts work aboard the ISS. Why don't they need space suits?

Space Fashion

Astronauts wear flight suits only for takeoff and landing. They wear regular clothes the rest of the time. They wear the same clothes for several days in a row. Spacecraft don't have washing machines. So dirty clothing is thrown away.

These astronauts do their work in casual shirts on the space shuttle *Discovery*.

This astronaut shows off some fresh fruit aboard the ISS.

Space Meals

Being weightless is part of the fun of space travel. But it can be tricky. An astronaut can't just set down a book or a spoon. Those objects will float away. Everything has to be strapped down or stuck to something else.

Astronauts eat their meals with care. Loose crumbs can float into equipment. That can cause damage. Food comes in sealed packages. Drinks stay in closed plastic pouches. The pouches have small openings for straws.

Eating a meal in space can be a challenge. Anything that isn't strapped down will float away.

Relaxing in Space

Astronauts sleep in sleeping bags. The sleeping bags are strapped to a wall or a seat. The straps keep astronauts from floating around all night.

Spacecraft have seats for takeoff and landing. But they don't have any chairs. Astronauts often use footholds when they eat or work. They slip their feet under straps or bars on the floor.

These astronauts are ready for some rest in their sleeping bags.

Chapter 5

TRAINING FOR SPACE

Thousands of people sign up to become astronauts. But few are chosen for the job. They must be strong and healthy. They must have studied math or science at a college. And they must go through years of training.

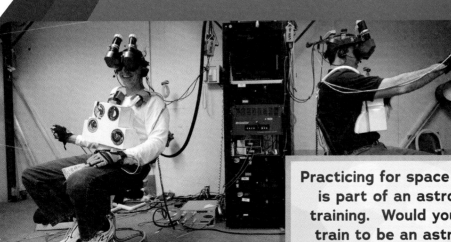

Practicing for space missions is part of an astronaut's training. Would you like to train to be an astronaut?

Astronauts in training learn how to live in space. They practice what to do in emergencies. They spend many hours in classrooms. They must prove that they are ready for space travel.

This astronaut practices an emergency exit from a space shuttle.

Practice Makes Perfect

Astronauts train on simulators. These life-size models act like real spacecraft. But they never leave the ground. Astronauts can practice flying and using a spacecraft's controls.

These Russian space travelers go over launch instructions for the Soyuz.

Training for Weightlessness

Astronauts also prepare to be weightless. They train underwater. Floating underwater is a lot like being weightless.

U.S. astronauts take flights in a special airplane too. The plane flies up high and then drops at high speeds. The falling creates a feeling of weightlessness. It can also make astronauts feel sick. That's why they call the plane the Vomit Comet!

ABOVE: **This astronaut is underwater, practicing for a space walk.**
LEFT: **The airplane called the Vomit Comet takes a dive through the clouds.**

High-G Training

High g-forces are hard on the body. So astronauts prepare. They train inside a centrifuge. This machine spins at very high speeds. It creates high g-forces.

This Canadian astronaut is ready to train in a Russian centrifuge.

Chapter 6

THE FUTURE OF SPACE TRAVEL

Astronauts aren't just explorers. They're scientists. They study how plants grow in space. They learn how animals behave.

Tending plants for experiments is one of the many jobs of astronauts on the ISS. How do astronauts' experiments help improve space travel?

Astronauts do tests on themselves. They learn how being weightless changes people's bodies. This work helps make space travel safer. It allows astronauts to stay in space for longer periods of time. And it helps with plans for future space travel.

Astronauts learn how the body reacts to space travel. Their experiments may help future astronauts.

Future Challenges

Someday astronauts may return to the Moon. Or they may travel to Mars. A trip to Mars would take more than a year!

In the future, people could even take vacations in space. A few people have paid to go into space. But not many people can afford such a trip.

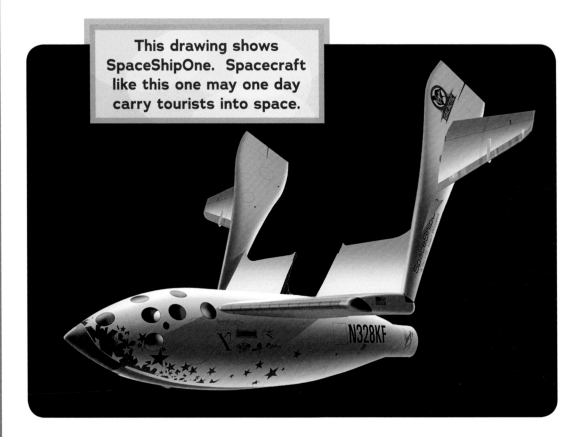

This drawing shows SpaceShipOne. Spacecraft like this one may one day carry tourists into space.

Some companies want to bring more people to space. They are building their own spacecraft. One day, they might even build space stations.

Would you like to take a space vacation? Maybe you'd rather be an astronaut. In the future, there may be many ways to explore outer space.

The astronaut and the spacecraft in this drawing have just landed on Mars. Might people travel to Mars in the future?

Glossary

air pressure: the force of air pressing against a person or an object

astronaut: a person trained to travel in space

centrifuge: a machine that quickly spins astronauts in circles to create high g-forces

friction: resistance caused by materials rubbing together

g-force: the feeling of weight caused by acceleration

gravity: a force that pulls objects together

heat shield: a protective layer on a reentry module that protects the module from the intense heat of reentry

module: a section of a spacecraft or space station

oxygen: a gas that people need for breathing

SAFER: Simplified Aid for EVA (extravehicular activity) Rescue. The SAFER is a machine that straps to the back of a space suit. It can shoot jets of air that fly a person a short distance in space.

simulator: a machine that models a spacecraft. Astronauts can practice flying on a simulator before they fly a real spacecraft.

Soyuz: a type of Russian spacecraft

spacecraft: a vehicle that carries people and supplies to outer space

space shuttle: a type of American spacecraft that was in use from 1981 until 2011

space walk: the job of moving and working outside in space

Learn More about Space Travel

Books

McCarthy, Meghan. *Astronaut Handbook*. New York: Alfred A. Knopf, 2008. Follow four future astronauts as they go through training.

Somervill, Barbara A. *The History of Space Travel*. Chanhassen, MN: Child's World, 2005. The author explores the past, present, and future of space travel.

Waxman, Laura Hamilton. *Exploring the International Space Station*. Minneapolis: Lerner Publications Company, 2012. This book explores the work of building and running the space station.

Websites

Clickable Spacesuit
http://www.nasa.gov/audience/foreducators/spacesuits/home/clickable_suit.html
Learn about everything a space walker needs to stay safe.

NASA Kids' Club
http://www.nasa.gov/audience/forkids/kidsclub/flash/index.html
This website is full of information, pictures, and activities related to space travel.

Station Spacewalk Game
http://www.nasa.gov/multimedia/3d_resources/station_spacewalk_game.html
Find out how hard it can be to build the International Space Station by playing this online game.

Index

Photo Acknowledgments

The images in this book are used with the permission of: NASA/KSC, pp. 4, 8, 10; © RIA Novosti/ Photo Researchers, Inc., pp. 5, 31; NASA, pp. 6, 7, 12, 15, 22, 23, 24, 25, 26, 27, 28, 32 (top), 35; © Stan Honda/AFP/Getty Images, p. 9; © Bruce Weaver/AFP/Getty Images, p. 11; NASA/Bill Ingalls, p. 13; REUTERS/Sergei Remezov, pp. 14, 33; © Adam Hart-Davis/Photo Researchers, Inc., p. 16; AP Photo/Maxim Shipenkov, p. 17; AP Photo/NASA TV, p. 18; AP Photo/NASA, p. 19; NASA/Kim Shiflett, p. 20; © Laura Westlund/Independent Picture Service, p. 21; © Science Source/Photo Researchers, Inc., pp. 29, 34; NASA/JSC, pp. 30, 32 (bottom); © Detlev van Ravenswaay/Photo Researchers, Inc., pp. 36, 37.
Front cover: NASA/Bill Ingalls.

Main body text set in Adrianna Regular 14/20
Typeface provided by Chank